DUMP
CAN SECRETS

pil

Publications International, Ltd.

Pictured on the front cover *(clockwise from top left):* Easy Lemon Cheesecake *(page 120)*,
Spicy Italian Sausage & Penne Pasta *(page 33)*, Tamale Pie Dip
(page 5), and Summer Fiesta Casserole *(page 44)*.

Pictured on the back cover *(left to right):* Southwestern Mac and Cheese
(page 50), Ramen Joy *(page 115)*, and Basil Cannellini Dip *(page 10)*.

ISBN: 978-1-68022-238-8

Library of Congress Control Number: 2015949950

Manufactured in China.

8 7 6 5 4 3 2 1

Microwave Cooking: Microwave ovens vary in wattage. Use the cooking times
as guidelines and check for doneness before adding more time

Preparation/Cooking Times: Preparation times are based on the approximate amount of time required
to assemble the recipe before cooking, baking, chilling or serving. These times include preparation
steps such as measuring, chopping and mixing. The fact that some preparations and cooking can be
done simultaneously is taken into account. Preparation of optional ingredients and serving suggestions
is not included.

CONTENTS

PARTY STARTERS

TAMALE PIE DIP

1 package (8 ounces) cream cheese

2 cups (8 ounces) shredded Mexican-style cheese, divided

1 can (8 ounces) creamed corn

1 can (8 ounces) diced tomatoes

½ cup sour cream

2 cloves garlic, minced

1 teaspoon chili powder

2 cups diced cooked chicken

1 teaspoon olive oil

Optional toppings: sour cream, sliced or chopped black olives, diced avocado, sliced green onions or diced tomato

Tortilla chips

1. Preheat oven to 325°F. Coat 9-inch quiche dish or deep-dish pie plate with nonstick cooking spray; set aside.

2. Process cream cheese, 1 cup Mexican-style cheese, corn, tomatoes, sour cream, garlic and chili powder in food processor or blender until almost smooth. Stir in chicken by hand. Spoon mixture into prepared dish. Top with remaining 1 cup Mexican-style cheese. Drizzle with oil. Bake 45 minutes.

3. Garnish with toppings as desired. Serve with tortilla chips.

Makes about 5 cups

EASY TACO DIP

½ pound ground beef
1 cup frozen corn
½ cup chopped onion
½ cup salsa
½ cup mild taco sauce
1 can (4 ounces) diced mild green chiles, drained
1 can (4 ounces) sliced black olives, drained
1 cup (4 ounces) shredded Mexican cheese blend
  Sour cream (optional)
  Tortilla chips

SLOW COOKER DIRECTIONS

1. Brown beef in large skillet over medium-high heat 6 to 8 minutes, stirring to break up meat. Drain fat. Transfer beef to slow cooker.

2. Add corn, onion, salsa, taco sauce, chiles and olives to slow cooker; mix well. Cover; cook on LOW 2 to 3 hours.

3. Just before serving, stir in cheese blend. Top with sour cream, if desired. Serve with tortilla chips.

Makes about 3 cups

TIP: To keep this dip hot through an entire party, simply leave it in the slow cooker on LOW or WARM.

HOT ARTICHOKE DIP

PREP TIME: 5 minutes   **BAKE TIME:** 30 minutes

1 envelope LIPTON®
   RECIPE SECRETS®
   Onion Soup Mix*

1 can (14 ounces)
   artichoke hearts,
   drained and
   chopped

1 cup HELLMANN'S® or
   BEST FOODS® Real
   Mayonnaise

1 container (8 ounces)
   sour cream

1 cup shredded Swiss
   or mozzarella cheese
   (about 4 ounces)

*Also terrific with LIPTON®
RECIPE SECRETS® Savory
Herb with Garlic, Golden Onion
or Onion Mushroom Soup Mix.*

1. Preheat oven to 350°F. In 1-quart casserole, combine all ingredients.

2. Bake uncovered, 30 minutes or until heated through.

3. Serve with your favorite dippers.

Makes 3 cups dip

COLD ARTICHOKE DIP: Omit Swiss cheese. Stir in, if desired, ¼ cup grated Parmesan cheese. Do not bake.

 TIP: When serving hot dip for a party, try baking it in 2 smaller casseroles. When the first casserole is empty, replace it with the second one, fresh from the oven.

BASIL CANNELLINI DIP

1 can (about 15 ounces) cannellini or Great Northern beans
1 clove garlic
2 tablespoons extra virgin olive oil
3 tablespoons chopped fresh basil
Salt and black pepper

1. Drain beans, reserving ¼ cup liquid. Rinse and drain beans.

2. With motor running, drop garlic clove through feed tube of food processor; process until finely chopped. Stop processor; add beans, reserved liquid and oil. Process until smooth.

3. Stir in basil. Season with salt and pepper.

Makes about 1½ cups

TIP: Serve with fresh vegetables or sliced French bread for dipping. Add 2 tablespoons fresh lemon juice with the basil for extra flavor.

CHUNKY HAWAIIAN

1   can (8 ounces) DOLE®
    Crushed Pineapple,
    well drained

½   cup fat free or light
    sour cream

1   package (3 ounces)
    light cream cheese,
    softened

¼   cup mango chutney*
    Low fat crackers
    (optional)

*If there are large pieces of fruit
in chutney, cut them into small
pieces.

BEAT crushed pineapple, sour cream, cream cheese and chutney in bowl until blended. Cover and chill 1 hour or overnight. Serve with crackers, if desired. Refrigerate any leftover spread in airtight container for up to one week.

Makes 2½ cups spread

CREAMY CHIPOTLE REFRIED BEAN DIP

1 tablespoon vegetable oil

1 small red onion, chopped (reserve ¼ cup for garnish)

1 can (15 ounces) fat-free refried beans

⅓ cup WISH-BONE® Chipotle Ranch Dressing

1 cup finely shredded romaine lettuce leaves

1 medium tomato, seeded and chopped

1. Heat oil in large nonstick skillet over medium heat and cook onion, stirring occasionally, 5 minutes or until tender. Stir in beans and cook, stirring frequently, 3 minutes or until heated through.

2. Turn into shallow 1½-quart serving dish or pie plate. Evenly spread WISH-BONE® Chipotle Ranch Dressing over beans, then top with lettuce, tomato and reserved onion. Drizzle, if desired, with additional Dressing.

Makes 3¼ cups

TIP: Chopped avocados are a great addition to this delicious dip!

BUFFALO CHICKEN DIP

2 (8-ounce) packages cream cheese, softened

1 cup ranch salad dressing

¾ cup hot buffalo sauce

1½ cups shredded Cheddar cheese

2 (10-ounce) cans HORMEL® Premium Chicken Breast, drained

Crackers, tortilla chips, bread and celery sticks

1. Heat oven to 400°F. In large bowl, combine cream cheese, dressing, hot sauce and shredded cheese until well blended. Gently stir in chicken.

2. Spoon dip into 2-quart casserole. Bake 20 minutes or until hot and bubbly. Serve with crackers, tortilla chips, bread and celery sticks for dipping.

Makes 8 servings

SLOW COOKER CHEESE DIP

1 pound ground beef

1 pound bulk Italian sausage

1 package (16 ounces) pasteurized process cheese product, cubed

1 can (11 ounces) sliced jalapeño peppers, drained*

1 onion, diced

2 cups (8 ounces) Cheddar cheese, cubed

1 package (8 ounces) cream cheese, cubed

1 container (8 ounces) cottage cheese

1 container (8 ounces) sour cream

1 can (8 ounces) diced tomatoes, drained

3 cloves garlic, minced

Salt and black pepper

Tortilla chips or crackers

*Jalapeño peppers can sting and irritate the skin, so wear rubber gloves when handling peppers and do not touch your eyes.

SLOW COOKER DIRECTIONS

1. Brown ground beef and sausage in medium skillet over medium-high heat 6 to 8 minutes, stirring to break up meat. Drain fat. Transfer meat to slow cooker.

2. Add cheese product, jalapeño peppers, onion, Cheddar cheese, cream cheese, cottage cheese, sour cream, tomatoes and garlic to slow cooker. Season with salt and black pepper.

3. Cover; cook on HIGH 1½ to 2 hours or until cheeses are melted. Serve with tortilla chips.

Makes 16 to 18 servings

BREAKFAST & BRUNCH

LEMON RASPBERRY OVEN PANCAKE

PREP TIME: 10 minutes   **BAKING TIME:** 15 minutes

½ cup all-purpose flour

¼ cup *plus* 2 tablespoons granulated sugar, *divided*

¼ teaspoon salt

1 can (12 fluid ounces) NESTLÉ® CARNATION® Evaporated Lowfat 2% Milk

¾ cup egg substitute or 3 large eggs

1½ teaspoons grated lemon peel

1 teaspoon vanilla extract

½ pint (about 1 cup) fresh raspberries

PREHEAT oven to 450°F.

SPRAY 9-inch deep-dish pie plate or cake pan with nonstick cooking spray.

COMBINE flour, ¼ *cup* sugar and salt in medium bowl. Whisk evaporated milk, egg substitute, lemon peel and vanilla extract in another medium bowl until blended. Add to flour mixture; whisk for 30 seconds or until smooth. Pour batter into prepared pie plate. Arrange raspberries on top of batter. Sprinkle top with *remaining 2 tablespoons* sugar.

BAKE for 15 to 20 minutes or until puffed and light golden brown. Serve warm.

Makes 8 servings

TIP: Substitute other fresh, seasonal berries such as blackberries or blueberries for the raspberries.

ITALIAN PUMPKIN STRATA

PREP TIME: 20 minutes   **BAKING TIME:** 30 minutes

1   tablespoon vegetable oil
1   pound sweet Italian sausage, casings removed
1   small onion, chopped
½   cup chopped green bell pepper
½   cup chopped red bell pepper
2   cloves garlic, finely chopped
12   cups (about 1 pound loaf) 1½-inch cubes Italian or French bread
2   cups (8 ounces) shredded mozzarella cheese
2   cans (12 fluid ounces *each*) NESTLÉ® CARNATION® Evaporated Milk
1   can (15 ounces) LIBBY'S® 100% Pure Pumpkin
4   large eggs
1   teaspoon salt
½   teaspoon ground black pepper
½   teaspoon dried oregano, crushed
½   teaspoon dried basil, crushed
½   teaspoon dried marjoram, crushed

PREHEAT oven to 350°F. Grease 13×9-inch baking pan.

HEAT oil in large skillet over medium-high heat. Add sausage, onion, bell peppers and garlic. Cook, stirring to break up sausage, for 7 to 10 minutes or until sausage is no longer pink; drain.

COMBINE bread cubes, cheese and sausage mixture in a large bowl. Beat evaporated milk, pumpkin, eggs, salt, pepper, oregano, basil and marjoram in medium bowl. Pour over bread mixture, stirring gently to moisten bread. Pour into prepared baking pan.

BAKE for 30 to 35 minutes or until set. Serve warm.

Makes 12 servings

YUMMY FRUIT SMOOTHIE

PREP TIME: 5 minutes

3   cups assorted
     fresh fruit (such
     as bananas,
     strawberries, mango,
     papaya, pineapple)

1   can (12 fluid
     ounces) NESTLÉ®
     CARNATION®
     Evaporated Milk,
     chilled

½   cup crushed ice

1   to 2 tablespoons
     granulated sugar
     (optional)

PLACE fruit, evaporated milk and ice in blender; cover. Blend until smooth. Taste; add sugar if needed.

Makes 4 servings

VARIATION: May substitute 3 cups cut-up frozen, unsweetened fruit or canned fruit for the fresh fruit. If using frozen fruit, thaw slightly and cut into smaller pieces. Crushed ice may not be needed. For canned fruit, drain and reserve juice or syrup. Substitute juice or syrup for sugar, if needed.

HASH BROWN BREAKFAST CASSEROLE

3 cups refrigerated or frozen hash brown potatoes, thawed

1½ cups (6 ounces) finely chopped extra-lean ham

¾ cup (3 ounces) shredded reduced-fat Cheddar cheese

¼ cup sliced green onions

1 can (12 ounces) evaporated fat-free (skim) milk

1 tablespoon all-purpose flour

1 cup cholesterol-free egg substitute

½ teaspoon black pepper

1. Lightly spray 8-inch square baking dish with nonstick cooking spray. Layer potatoes, ham, cheese and green onions in prepared dish.

2. Gradually whisk evaporated milk into flour in medium bowl. Stir in egg substitute and pepper; pour over potato mixture. Cover; refrigerate 4 hours or overnight.

3. Preheat oven to 350°F. Bake, uncovered, 55 to 60 minutes or until knife inserted into center comes out clean. Let stand 10 minutes before serving.

Makes 6 servings

PUMPKIN GRANOLA

3 cups old-fashioned oats

¾ cup coarsely chopped almonds

¾ cup raw pumpkin seeds (pepitas)

½ cup canned pumpkin

½ cup maple syrup

⅓ cup coconut oil, melted

1 teaspoon vanilla

1 teaspoon ground cinnamon

½ teaspoon salt

¼ teaspoon ground ginger

¼ teaspoon ground nutmeg

Pinch ground cloves

¾ cup dried cranberries

1. Preheat oven to 325°F. Line large rimmed baking sheet with parchment paper.

2. Combine oats, almonds and pumpkin seeds in large bowl. Combine pumpkin, maple syrup, oil, vanilla, cinnamon, salt, ginger, nutmeg and cloves in medium bowl; stir until well blended. Pour over oat mixture; stir until well blended and all ingredients are completely coated. Spread mixture evenly on prepared baking sheet.

3. Bake 50 to 60 minutes or until granola is golden brown and no longer moist, stirring every 20 minutes. (Granola will become more crisp as it cools.) Stir in cranberries; cool completely.

Makes about 5½ cups

VARIATIONS: For Pumpkin Chocolate Granola, follow recipe above but reduce amount of maple syrup to ⅓ cup. Stir in ¾ cup semisweet chocolate chips after baking. You can substitute pecans or walnuts for the almonds, and/or add ¾ cup flaked coconut to the mixture before baking.

BERRY SMOOTHIE

PREP TIME: 5 minutes

1 ripe, medium DOLE®
Banana, peeled

1 can (6 ounces) **or**
¾ cup DOLE®
Pineapple Juice

1 carton (6 ounces)
blueberry **or** mixed
berries yogurt

1 cup DOLE® Frozen
Blueberries, partially
thawed

COMBINE banana, pineapple juice, yogurt and blueberries in blender or food processor container. Cover; blend until smooth.

Makes 3 servings

PUMPKIN POWER SMOOTHIE

⅓ cup water

1 sweet red apple, seeded and cut into chunks

½ frozen banana

½ cup canned pumpkin

½ cup ice cubes

1 tablespoon lemon juice

1 tablespoon ground flaxseed

1 teaspoon honey

Dash ground nutmeg

Combine water, apple, banana, pumpkin, ice, lemon juice, flaxseed, honey and nutmeg in blender; blend until smooth. Serve immediately.

Makes 1 serving

BAKED PUMPKIN FRENCH TOAST

1 tablespoon butter, softened

1 loaf challah or egg bread (12 to 16 ounces), cut into ¾-inch-thick slices

7 eggs

1¼ cups whole milk

⅔ cup canned pumpkin

1 teaspoon vanilla

½ teaspoon pumpkin pie spice

⅛ teaspoon salt

3 tablespoons sugar

2 teaspoons ground cinnamon

Maple syrup

1. Generously grease 13×9-inch baking dish with butter. Arrange bread slices in dish, fitting slices in tightly.

2. Combine eggs, milk, pumpkin, vanilla, pumpkin pie spice and salt in medium bowl; beat until well blended. Pour over bread in baking dish; turn slices to coat completely with egg mixture. Cover and refrigerate 8 hours or overnight.

3. Preheat oven to 350°F. Combine sugar and cinnamon in small bowl; mix well. Turn bread slices again; sprinkle generously with cinnamon-sugar.

4. Bake about 30 minutes or until bread is puffy and golden brown. Serve immediately with maple syrup.

Makes 6 servings

HASH BROWN CASSEROLE WITH BACON

1 package (32 ounces) frozen Southern-style hash brown potatoes, thawed

1 container (16 ounces) sour cream

1 can (10¾ ounces) condensed cream of chicken soup

1½ cups (6 ounces) shredded sharp Cheddar cheese

¾ cup thinly sliced green onions

4 slices bacon, crisp-cooked and crumbled

2 teaspoons hot pepper sauce

¼ teaspoon garlic salt

1. Preheat oven to 350°F. Spray 13×9-inch baking pan with nonstick cooking spray.

2. Combine potatoes, sour cream, soup, cheese, green onions, bacon, hot pepper sauce and garlic salt in large bowl. Spoon evenly into prepared dish.

3. Bake 55 to 60 minutes or until potatoes are tender and cooked through. Stir before serving.

Makes 6 servings

BREAKFAST BEANS AND RICE

1 package (10 ounces) frozen brown rice

2 tablespoons extra virgin olive oil, divided

1 cup diced onions

1 medium poblano chile pepper, seeded and diced

½ of a 15-ounce can black beans, rinsed and drained

1 cup seeded diced tomatoes

¼ cup chopped fresh cilantro

2 teaspoons paprika

½ to ¾ teaspoon salt

1 lime, quartered

1. Cook rice according to package directions.

2. Meanwhile, heat 1 tablespoon oil in large nonstick skillet over medium-high heat. Cook and stir onions and poblano pepper 4 to 5 minutes or until lightly browned. Add beans, tomatoes, cilantro, paprika and salt. Cook and stir 30 seconds. Remove from heat. Stir in rice and remaining oil; squeeze lime wedges over each serving.

Makes 4 servings

LUNCH & DINNER

SPICY ITALIAN SAUSAGE & PENNE PASTA

- 8 ounces uncooked penne pasta
- 1 pound bulk hot Italian sausage
- 1 cup chopped sweet onion
- 2 cloves garlic, minced
- 2 cans (about 14 ounces each) seasoned diced tomatoes
- 3 cups broccoli florets
- ½ cup shredded Asiago or Romano cheese

1. Cook pasta according to package directions; drain. Return to saucepan; keep warm.

2. Meanwhile, crumble sausage into large skillet. Add onion; cook and stir over medium-high heat until sausage is cooked through. Drain fat. Add garlic; cook 1 minute. Stir in tomatoes and broccoli. Cover; cook 10 minutes or until broccoli is tender.

3. Add sausage mixture to pasta; toss to coat. Sprinkle with Asiago cheese.

Makes 4 to 6 servings

 TIP: To add extra flavor to pasta dishes, slice fresh basil leaves into thin shreds. Sprinkle basil over pasta just before serving.

TUSCAN TURKEY AND WHITE BEAN SKILLET

1   **teaspoon dried rosemary, divided**

½   **teaspoon garlic salt**

½   **teaspoon black pepper, divided**

1   **pound turkey breast cutlets, pounded to ¼-inch thickness**

2   **teaspoons canola oil**

1   **can (about 15 ounces) navy beans or Great Northern beans, rinsed and drained**

1   **can (about 14 ounces) fire-roasted diced tomatoes**

¼   **cup grated Parmesan cheese**

1. Combine ½ teaspoon rosemary, garlic salt and ¼ teaspoon pepper in small bowl; mix well. Sprinkle over turkey.

2. Heat oil in large nonstick skillet over medium heat. Add turkey; cook 2 to 3 minutes per side or until no longer pink in center.

3. Add beans, tomatoes, remaining ½ teaspoon rosemary and ¼ teaspoon pepper to skillet; bring to a boil over high heat. Reduce heat to low; simmer 5 minutes.

4. Spoon bean mixture over turkey; sprinkle with cheese.

Makes 6 servings

CREAMY CHICKEN

3   boneless skinless chicken breasts *or* 6 boneless skinless chicken thighs

2   cans (10¾ ounces each) condensed cream of chicken soup, undiluted

1   can (about 14 ounces) chicken broth

1   can (4 ounces) sliced mushrooms, drained

½   medium onion, diced

Salt

Black pepper

Hot cooked wide egg noodles (optional)

SLOW COOKER DIRECTIONS

Place all ingredients except salt and pepper in slow cooker. Cover; cook on LOW 6 to 8 hours. Season to taste with salt and pepper. Serve over noodles, if desired.

Makes 3 servings

 TIP: If desired, you may add 8 ounces of cubed pasteurized process cheese spread before serving.

CHEESY TUNA MAC

8   ounces uncooked
    elbow macaroni

2   tablespoons
    margarine or butter

2   tablespoons
    all-purpose flour

1   teaspoon paprika

¼   teaspoon salt

1   cup canned chicken
    broth

6   ounces pasteurized
    process cheese
    product, cut into
    cubes

1   can (6 ounces) tuna
    packed in water,
    drained and flaked

1. Cook macaroni according to package directions, omitting salt. Drain; set aside.

2. Melt margarine in medium saucepan over medium heat. Add flour, paprika and salt; cook and stir 1 minute. Add broth; bring to a simmer for 2 minutes or until sauce thickens.

3. Add cheese product; cook and stir until melted. Combine tuna and pasta in medium bowl; pour sauce mixture over tuna mixture; toss to coat. Sprinkle with additional paprika.

Makes 4 servings

RAINBOW CASSEROLE

5 potatoes, peeled and cut into thin slices

1 pound ground beef

1 onion, halved and thinly sliced

1 can (about 28 ounces) stewed tomatoes, drained, juice reserved

1 cup frozen peas *or* 1 can (about 6 ounces) peas, drained

Salt and black pepper

1. Preheat oven to 350°F. Lightly coat 3-quart casserole with nonstick cooking spray.

2. Combine potatoes and enough water to cover in large saucepan; bring to a boil over high heat. Reduce heat to low; simmer 15 minutes or until almost tender. Drain. Meanwhile, brown beef in large skillet over medium-high heat 6 to 8 minutes, stirring to break up meat. Drain fat.

3. Layer beef, potatoes, onion, tomatoes, peas, salt and pepper in prepared casserole. Add reserved tomato juice.

4. Bake, covered, 40 minutes or until most liquid is absorbed.

Makes 4 to 6 servings

SHREDDED BEEF FAJITAS

1   beef flank steak (about 1 pound), cut into 6 portions

1   can (about 14 ounces) diced tomatoes with mild green chiles

1   cup chopped onion

½   medium green bell pepper, cut into ½-inch pieces

1   clove garlic, minced or ¼ teaspoon garlic powder

½   package (about 2 tablespoons) fajita seasoning mix

6   (8-inch) flour tortillas

Optional toppings: sour cream, guacamole, shredded Cheddar cheese, salsa

SLOW COOKER DIRECTIONS

1. Place beef in 3½-quart slow cooker. Combine tomatoes with juice, onion, bell pepper, garlic and fajita seasoning mix in medium bowl. Pour over beef. Cover; cook on LOW 8 to 10 hours or on HIGH 4 to 5 hours or until beef is tender.

2. Remove beef to cutting board; shred with two forks. Return beef to slow cooker and stir.

3. To serve fajitas, place meat mixture evenly into tortillas. Add toppings as desired; roll up tortillas.

Makes 6 servings

TURKEY SAUSAGE & PASTA TOSS

8 ounces uncooked penne or gemelli pasta

1 can (about 14 ounces) stewed tomatoes

6 ounces turkey kielbasa or smoked turkey sausage, cut crosswise into ¼-inch-thick slices

2 cups (1-inch) fresh asparagus pieces or broccoli florets

2 tablespoons prepared pesto

2 tablespoons grated Parmesan cheese

1. Cook pasta according to package directions, omitting salt. Drain.

2. Meanwhile, heat tomatoes in medium saucepan. Add sausage, asparagus and pesto; cover and simmer about 6 minutes or until asparagus is crisp-tender.

3. Toss cooked pasta with tomato mixture; sprinkle with cheese.

Makes 4 servings

CHICKEN, RICE AND BEAN SKILLET

1 to 2 tablespoons olive oil

4 boneless skinless chicken breasts (about 4 ounces each)

2 cups water

1 can (about 14 ounces) Mexican-style diced tomatoes

1 box (8 ounces) red beans and rice mix

1. Heat oil in large skillet over medium-high heat. Add chicken; cook until no longer pink in center.

2. Add water, tomatoes with juice and rice and beans mix; bring mixture to a boil. Reduce heat to low and simmer 20 to 25 minutes or until most liquid has absorbed.

Makes 4 servings

SUMMER FIESTA CASSEROLE

2 pounds ground beef

1 medium onion, chopped

1 package (about 1 ounce) taco seasoning mix

4 to 6 potatoes, peeled and cut into ½-inch cubes (about 4 cups)

1 to 2 tablespoons vegetable oil

4 cups sliced zucchini

1 can (about 14 ounces) diced tomatoes with onion and garlic

1½ cups (6 ounces) shredded Mexican cheese blend

1. Preheat oven to 350°F. Spray 4-quart casserole with nonstick cooking spray.

2. Brown beef and onion in large skillet over medium heat 6 to 8 minutes, stirring to break up meat. Drain fat. Add taco seasoning and cook 5 minutes, stirring occasionally. Transfer meat mixture to prepared casserole.

3. Add potatoes to same skillet; cook and stir over medium heat until potatoes are browned, adding oil as needed to prevent sticking. Add zucchini; cook and stir until beginning to soften. Transfer to casserole; top with tomatoes and cheese.

4. Bake 10 to 15 minutes or until cheese is melted and casserole is heated through.

Makes 4 to 6 servings

TIP: Serve with tortilla chips, sour cream and/or salsa.

TUNA SALAD STUFFED SWEET RED PEPPERS

2   cans (5 ounces each) albacore tuna packed in water, drained and flaked

2   large stalks celery, sliced diagonally

½   cup halved green grapes

½   cup (2 ounces) shredded sharp Cheddar cheese

⅓   cup mayonnaise

Salt and black pepper

2   red bell peppers, halved and seeded

1. Combine tuna, celery, grapes, cheese and mayonnaise in medium bowl; mix well. Season with salt and black pepper.

2. Divide tuna mixture evenly among hollowed bell pepper halves.

Makes 4 servings

DOUBLE-QUICK MOZZARELLA CHICKEN

4 boneless skinless chicken breasts (about 1 pound)

Juice of ½ medium lemon or lime

1 teaspoon ground cumin

¼ teaspoon salt

¾ cup (3 ounces) shredded mozzarella cheese

½ of a 10-ounce can Mexican-style diced tomatoes with mild green chiles,* drained

2 tablespoons chopped fresh cilantro (optional)

Reserve remaining tomatoes and juice for another use.

1. Preheat oven to 400°F. Line baking sheet with foil. Arrange chicken breasts about 2 inches apart. Drizzle lemon juice over chicken. Sprinkle with cumin and salt. Bake 20 minutes.

2. Sprinkle cheese evenly over chicken; bake 5 minutes or until chicken is no longer pink in center. Transfer to serving platter. Spoon about 3 tablespoons diced tomatoes over each chicken breast. Sprinkle with cilantro.

Makes 4 servings

SERVING SUGGESTION: This dish is excellent served with ½ cup cooked egg noodles, fried yellow squash and onions, or green beans.

TUNA TOMATO CASSEROLE

2 cans (6 ounces each) tuna, drained and flaked

1 cup mayonnaise

1 onion, finely chopped

¼ teaspoon salt

¼ teaspoon black pepper

1 package (12 ounces) wide egg noodles, uncooked

8 to 10 plum tomatoes, sliced ¼ inch thick

1 cup (4 ounces) shredded Cheddar or mozzarella cheese

1. Preheat oven to 375°F.

2. Combine tuna, mayonnaise, onion, salt and pepper in medium bowl; mix well.

3. Cook noodles according to package directions. Drain and return to saucepan. Stir tuna mixture into noodles until well blended.

4. Layer noodle mixture, tomatoes and cheese in 13×9-inch baking dish. Press down slightly.

5. Bake 20 minutes or until cheese is melted and casserole is heated through.

Makes 6 servings

SOUTHWESTERN MAC AND CHEESE

1 package (8 ounces) elbow macaroni, uncooked

1 can (about 14 ounces) diced tomatoes with green peppers and onions

1 can (10 ounces) diced tomatoes with mild green chiles

1½ cups salsa

3 cups (about 12 ounces) shredded Mexican cheese blend, divided

SLOW COOKER DIRECTIONS

1. Lightly coat inside of slow cooker with nonstick cooking spray. Stir together macaroni, tomatoes with juice, salsa and 2 cups cheese in slow cooker. Cover; cook on LOW 3 hours 45 minutes or until macaroni is tender.

2. Sprinkle remaining 1 cup cheese over contents of slow cooker. Cover; cook on LOW 15 minutes or until cheese is melted.

Makes 6 servings

ITALIAN BEEF RAGU

2 tablespoons olive oil

1 cup chopped onion

2 cans (about 14 ounces each) fire-roasted diced tomatoes

1 teaspoon dried oregano

1 teaspoon dried basil

⅛ teaspoon red pepper flakes or black pepper

1 package (about 17 ounces) fully cooked beef pot roast*

8 ounces uncooked fettuccine

*Fully cooked beef pot roast can be found in the refrigerated prepared meats section of the supermarket.

1. Heat oil in large saucepan over medium heat. Add onion; cook 5 minutes or until translucent and slightly browned, stirring occasionally. Add tomatoes, oregano, basil and red pepper flakes. Bring to a boil over high heat. Reduce heat to low; simmer 10 minutes, stirring occasionally.

2. Remove pot roast from package; add au jus to tomato mixture. Break meat into 1- to 1½-inch pieces. Add to tomato mixture; simmer 5 to 10 minutes or until heated through.

3. Cook fettuccine according to package directions; drain. Serve ragu over fettuccine.

Makes 4 servings

VEGETARIAN JAMBALAYA

1 **tablespoon vegetable oil**

½ **cup diced green or red bell pepper**

1 **can (about 14 ounces) diced tomatoes with mild green chiles**

1 **package (12 ounces) ground taco/burrito flavor soy meat substitute, crumbled**

1 **package (about 9 ounces) New Orleans style ready-to-serve jambalaya rice**

2 **tablespoons water**

1. Heat oil in large skillet over medium-high heat. Add bell pepper; cook and stir 3 minutes.

2. Add tomatoes, soy crumbles and rice; mix well. Stir in water. Cook 5 minutes, uncovered, or until heated through.

Makes 4 servings

SNAPPY HALIBUT SKILLET

½ tsp. thyme, crushed

1½ lb. halibut or other firm white fish

1 Tbsp. olive oil

1 onion, chopped

1 clove garlic, minced

1 Tbsp. cornstarch

1 can (14.5 oz.) DEL MONTE® Stewed Tomatoes, No Salt Added

¼ cup sliced green onions

1. Sprinkle thyme over both sides of fish. In large skillet, cook fish in hot oil over medium-high heat until fish flakes easily when tested with fork. Remove fish to plate; keep warm.

2. Cook chopped onion and garlic in same skillet until tender. Stir cornstarch into tomatoes; pour into skillet. Cook, stirring frequently, until thickened. Return fish to skillet; top with green onions. Heat through.

Makes 4 servings

HONEY-MUSTARD CHICKEN SALAD

4 ounces canned white meat chicken, rinsed and drained

½ cup sliced seedless red grapes

¼ cup chopped water chestnuts

2 tablespoons honey-mustard salad dressing

¼ teaspoon grated lemon peel

1 cup fresh spinach, washed, dried, stems removed

1 teaspoon pine nuts, toasted

⅛ teaspoon black pepper

1. Toss chicken, grapes, water chestnuts, salad dressing and lemon peel in small bowl until well coated. Let stand 5 minutes for dressing to absorb.

2. Arrange spinach on plate; place salad on top of spinach. Sprinkle pine nuts on top; season with pepper.

Makes 1 serving

EASY CHICKEN & MUSHROOM SKILLET

1 pound boneless skinless chicken breasts, cut into bite-size pieces

1 can (about 14 ounces) chicken broth

¼ cup hot water

½ teaspoon dried thyme

2 cups uncooked instant rice

8 ounces mushrooms, thinly sliced

1 can (10¾ ounces) cream of celery soup

Chopped fresh parsley

1. Cook chicken in broth and water in 12-inch nonstick skillet until mixture comes to a full boil. Stir in thyme and rice. Place mushrooms on top. (Do not stir mushrooms into rice.) Cover skillet; turn off heat and let stand 5 minutes.

2. Stir in soup; cook over low heat 5 minutes or until heated through. Sprinkle with parsley.

Makes 4 servings

BEEF MACARONI AND CHEESE

1 lb. lean ground beef

1 cup chopped onion

Salt and pepper (optional)

1 can (14.5 oz.) DEL MONTE® Diced Tomatoes with Basil, Garlic and Oregano

1 cup water

1 cup dry elbow macaroni

1½ cups shredded low-fat cheddar cheese

Light sour cream (optional)

1. Brown beef and onion over medium-high heat in skillet; drain. Season with salt and pepper, if desired.

2. Add undrained tomatoes and water; bring to boil.

3. Stir in dry macaroni. Cover and simmer 10 minutes or until tender.

4. Stir in cheese. Garnish with sour cream, if desired.

Makes 4 servings

MEXICAN CASSEROLE WITH TORTILLA CHIPS

12 ounces lean ground turkey

1 can (about 14 ounces) stewed tomatoes

½ of a 16-ounce package frozen bell pepper stir-fry blend, thawed

¾ teaspoon ground cumin

½ teaspoon salt

1½ ounces finely shredded sharp Cheddar cheese

2 ounces tortilla chips, lightly crushed

1. Spray large nonstick skillet with nonstick cooking spray. Cook turkey over medium heat until no longer pink, stirring to break up meat. Stir in tomatoes, bell peppers and cumin; bring to a boil. Reduce heat; cover and simmer 20 minutes or until vegetables are tender.

2. Stir in salt. Sprinkle evenly with cheese and chips.

Makes 4 servings

VARIATION: Sprinkle chips into a casserole. Spread cooked turkey mixture evenly over the chips and top with cheese.

CHICKEN COUSCOUS

½ pound boneless skinless chicken breasts, cut into 1-inch cubes

4 medium zucchini, sliced

1 can (about 14 ounces) diced tomatoes

1 can (about 14 ounces) chicken broth

1 teaspoon Italian seasoning

1 cup uncooked whole wheat couscous

1. Spray large skillet with nonstick cooking spray; heat over medium-high heat. Cook and stir chicken 4 minutes or until lightly browned.

2. Add zucchini, tomatoes, broth and Italian seasoning. Reduce heat to low; simmer 15 minutes, stirring occasionally.

3. Stir in couscous; remove from heat. Cover and let stand 7 minutes. Fluff with fork.

Makes 4 servings

CREOLE SHRIMP AND RICE

2 tablespoons olive oil

1 cup uncooked rice

1 can (about 14 ounces) diced tomatoes with garlic

1½ cups water

1 teaspoon Creole or Cajun seasoning blend

1 pound peeled cooked medium shrimp (with tails on)

1 package (10 ounces) frozen okra *or* 1½ cups frozen sugar snap peas, thawed

1. Heat oil in large skillet over medium heat. Add rice; cook and stir 2 to 3 minutes or until lightly browned.

2. Add tomatoes, water and Creole seasoning; bring to a boil. Reduce heat to medium-low; cover and simmer 15 minutes.

3. Add shrimp and okra; simmer, covered, 3 minutes or until heated through.

Makes 4 servings

NOTE: Okra are oblong green pods. When cooked, it gives off a viscous substance that acts as a good thickener.

STOVETOP TUNA CASSEROLE

1 package (12 ounces) deluxe macaroni and cheese dinner with shell pasta

2 cups frozen peas

1 tablespoon butter

1 can (about 6 ounces) chunk white tuna, drained and flaked

½ teaspoon black pepper (optional)

1. Remove cheese sauce pouch from macaroni and cheese; set aside. Bring 6 cups cold water to a boil in large saucepan. Stir in pasta. Cook 6 to 8 minutes or until pasta is tender.

2. Meanwhile, bring 4 cups cold water to a boil in medium saucepan. Stir in peas. Cook 3 to 5 minutes or until tender. Drain.

3. Drain pasta and return to saucepan. Stir in reserved cheese sauce, butter, tuna and peas; blend well. Sprinkle with pepper, if desired.

Makes 4 servings

VARIATION: Preheat oven to 350°F. Spray 8-inch baking dish with nonstick cooking spray. Spread tuna casserole mixture into prepared baking dish. Sprinkle with 1½ cups crushed potato chips or buttery round crackers. Bake 12 to 15 minutes or until topping is lightly browned.

TIP: Check your fridge for extra veggies to toss into this quick casserole. Stir in ¼ to ½ cup of the extra ingredient with the peas. Try one peeled and finely chopped carrot, or finely chopped green onions, red onions, mushrooms or celery.

SHRIMP AND CHICKEN PAELLA

¾ **cup cooked rice**

2 **cans (about 14 ounces each) diced tomatoes**

½ **teaspoon ground turmeric** *or* **⅛ teaspoon saffron threads**

1 **package (12 ounces) medium raw shrimp, peeled and deveined (with tails on)**

2 **chicken tenders (about 4 ounces), cut into 1-inch pieces**

1 **cup frozen peas**

1. Preheat oven to 400°F. Lightly coat 8-inch square baking dish with nonstick cooking spray. Spread rice in prepared dish.

2. Pour 1 can of tomatoes over rice; sprinkle with turmeric. Arrange shrimp and chicken over tomatoes; top with peas.

3. Drain remaining can of tomatoes, discarding juice. Spread tomatoes evenly over shrimp and chicken. Cover; bake 30 minutes. Let stand, covered, 5 minutes before serving. To serve, spoon into shallow bowls.

Makes 4 servings

SKILLET CHICKEN CREOLE

1 small red onion, chopped

1 small red bell pepper, chopped

1 jalapeño pepper,* seeded and minced

2 cups canned crushed tomatoes

¼ teaspoon salt

⅛ teaspoon black pepper

12 ounces boneless skinless chicken breasts, cut into strips

*Jalapeño peppers can sting and irritate the skin, so wear rubber gloves when handling peppers and do not touch your eyes.

1. Spray large nonstick skillet with nonstick cooking spray; heat over medium heat until hot. Add onion, bell pepper and jalapeño pepper; cook over medium heat 5 to 10 minutes or until vegetables are tender, stirring frequently. Stir in crushed tomatoes, salt and black pepper.

2. Stir in chicken. Reduce heat to low; cover and simmer 12 to 15 minutes or until chicken is cooked through.

Makes 4 servings

NOTE: If jalapeño pepper is too mild-tasting, add ¼ teaspoon red pepper flakes.

ROASTED SAUSAGE WITH WHITE BEANS

1 pound (4 links) Italian sausage

2 tablespoons extra virgin olive oil

10 fresh sage leaves (about 1 sprig)

2 cloves garlic, minced

1 can (about 14 ounces) diced tomatoes

2 cans (about 15 ounces each) cannellini beans, rinsed and drained

¼ teaspoon salt

⅛ teaspoon black pepper

1. Preheat oven to 400°F. Line rimmed baking sheet with foil. Arrange sausages on prepared baking sheet; roast about 18 minutes or until sausages are cooked through.

2. Meanwhile, heat oil in large skillet over medium-low heat. Add sage and garlic; cook 2 to 3 minutes or just until garlic begins to turn golden. Add tomatoes; bring to a simmer.

3. Stir in beans, salt and pepper; simmer about 15 minutes. Serve sausages over beans.

Makes 4 servings

NOTE: Sausages can be grilled instead of roasted.

SOUTH-OF-THE-BORDER MACARONI & CHEESE

5 cups cooked rotini pasta

2 cups (8 ounces) cubed American cheese

1 can (12 ounces) evaporated milk

1 cup (4 ounces) cubed sharp Cheddar cheese

1 can (4 ounces) diced mild green chiles, drained

2 teaspoons chili powder

2 medium tomatoes, seeded and chopped

5 green onions, sliced

SLOW COOKER DIRECTIONS

1. Combine pasta, American cheese, evaporated milk, Cheddar cheese, chiles and chili powder in slow cooker; mix well. Cover; cook on HIGH 2 hours, stirring occasionally.

2. Stir in tomatoes and green onions; continue cooking until heated through.

Makes 4 servings

SOUPS, STEWS & CHILIES

FEELIN' GOOD VEGETABLE SOUP

½ pound ground turkey or ground beef

1 can (about 14 ounces) chicken or beef broth

1 can (8 ounces) tomato sauce

½ cup uncooked small shell pasta

1 teaspoon chili powder or Cajun seasoning

½ teaspoon dried basil

⅛ teaspoon garlic powder

1½ cups frozen mixed vegetables

1. Brown turkey in medium saucepan over medium-high heat 6 to 8 minutes, stirring to break up meat. Drain fat. Stir in broth, tomato sauce, pasta, chili powder, basil and garlic powder. Bring to a boil over high heat. Reduce heat to low. Simmer, covered, 5 minutes.

2. Stir in frozen vegetables. Bring to a boil over high heat. Simmer, covered, 5 minutes or until pasta is tender.

Makes 4 servings

NEW ORLEANS FISH SOUP

1 can (about 15 ounces)
    cannellini beans,
    rinsed and drained

1 can (about 14 ounces)
    chicken broth

1 yellow squash, halved
    lengthwise and
    sliced (1 cup)

1 tablespoon Cajun
    seasoning

2 cans (about 14 ounces
    each) stewed
    tomatoes

1 pound skinless firm
    fish fillets, such as
    grouper, cod or
    haddock, cut into
    1-inch pieces

½ cup sliced green
    onions

1 teaspoon grated
    orange peel

1. Combine beans, broth, squash and
Cajun seasoning in large saucepan.
Bring to a boil over high heat.
Reduce heat to medium-low.

2. Stir in tomatoes and fish; cover
and simmer 3 to 5 minutes or until
fish begins to flake when tested
with fork. Stir in green onions and
orange peel.

Makes 4 servings

WEEKNIGHT CHILI

1 pound ground beef or turkey

1 package (1¼ ounces) chili seasoning mix

1 can (about 15 ounces) red kidney beans, rinsed and drained

1 can (about 14 ounces) diced tomatoes with mild green chiles

1 can (8 ounces) tomato sauce

1 cup (4 ounces) shredded Cheddar cheese

Sliced green onions (optional)

SLOW COOKER DIRECTIONS

1. Brown beef in large skillet over medium-high heat, stirring to break up meat. Drain fat. Stir in seasoning mix.

2. Place beef mixture, beans, tomatoes and tomato sauce in slow cooker. Cover; cook on LOW 4 to 6 hours. Top each serving with cheese and green onions.

Makes 4 servings

SWISS STEAK STEW

2 to 3 boneless beef top
  sirloin steaks (about
  4 pounds), cut into
  3 to 4 pieces

2 cans (about
  14 ounces each)
  diced tomatoes

2 green bell peppers,
  cut into ½-inch
  strips

2 onions, chopped

1 tablespoon seasoned
  salt

1 teaspoon black
  pepper

SLOW COOKER DIRECTIONS

Place steak in slow cooker. Add tomatoes, bell peppers and onions. Sprinkle with seasoned salt and black pepper. Cover; cook on LOW 8 hours or until beef is tender.

Makes 10 servings

 TIP: To increase the flavor of the finished dish and more closely follow the traditional preparation of Swiss steak, dust the steak pieces with flour and brown in a bit of olive oil in a large skillet over medium-high heat before adding them to the slow cooker.

QUICK TUSCAN BEAN, TOMATO AND SPINACH SOUP

- 2 cans (about 14 ounces each) diced tomatoes with onions
- 1 can (about 14 ounces) chicken broth
- 2 teaspoons sugar
- 2 teaspoons dried basil
- ¾ teaspoon Worcestershire sauce
- 1 can (about 15 ounces) small white beans, rinsed and drained
- 3 ounces fresh baby spinach leaves or chopped spinach leaves, stems removed
- 2 teaspoons extra virgin olive oil

1. Combine tomatoes, broth, sugar, basil and Worcestershire sauce in Dutch oven or large saucepan; bring to a boil over high heat. Reduce heat to low. Simmer, uncovered, 10 minutes.

2. Stir in beans and spinach; cook 5 minutes or until spinach is tender.

3. Remove from heat; stir in oil just before serving.

Makes 4 servings

AMERICA'S GARDEN SOUP

2 cans (14.5 oz. each) DEL MONTE® Diced Tomatoes with Basil, Garlic and Oregano-No Salt Added

2 cans (14.5 oz. each) DEL MONTE® Light & Fat Free Chicken Broth 50% Less Sodium

1 can (15.25 oz.) DEL MONTE® Whole Kernel Corn-No Salt Added

1 can (14.5 oz.) DEL MONTE® Cut Green Beans-No Salt Added

1 can (14.5 oz.) DEL MONTE® Zucchini with Italian Style Tomato Sauce

1 can (14.5 oz.) DEL MONTE® Whole New Potatoes, cut into cubes

1 can (8.25 oz.) DEL MONTE® Sliced Carrots

1. Drain liquid from all vegetables, except zucchini and tomatoes.

2. Combine all ingredients in 5-quart saucepan.

3. Bring to boil. Reduce heat and simmer 3 minutes.

Makes 10 servings

QUICK & EASY MEATBALL SOUP

1 package (15 to 18 ounces) frozen Italian sausage meatballs without sauce

2 cans (about 14 ounces each) Italian-style stewed tomatoes

2 cans (about 14 ounces each) beef broth

1 can (about 14 ounces) mixed vegetables

½ cup uncooked rotini pasta or small macaroni

½ teaspoon dried oregano

1. Thaw meatballs in microwave according to package directions.

2. Place tomatoes, broth, mixed vegetables, pasta and oregano in large saucepan. Add meatballs; bring to a boil over medium-high heat. Reduce heat to medium-low. Simmer, covered, 15 minutes or until pasta is tender.

Makes 4 to 6 servings

BLACK AND WHITE CHILI

1 pound chicken tenders, cut into ¾-inch pieces

1 cup coarsely chopped onion

1 can (about 15 ounces) Great Northern beans, drained

1 can (about 15 ounces) black beans, drained

1 can (about 14 ounces) Mexican-style stewed tomatoes, undrained

2 tablespoons Texas-style chili powder seasoning mix

SLOW COOKER DIRECTIONS

1. Spray large skillet with nonstick cooking spray; heat over medium heat until hot. Add chicken and onion; cook and stir 5 minutes or until chicken is browned.

2. Combine chicken mixture, beans, tomatoes and chili seasoning in slow cooker. Cover; cook on LOW 4 to 4½ hours.

Makes 6 servings

SERVING SUGGESTION: For a change of pace, this delicious chili is excellent served over cooked rice or pasta.

ITALIAN STEW

1   can (about 14 ounces) chicken broth

1   can (about 14 ounces) Italian stewed tomatoes with peppers and onions, undrained

1   package (9 ounces) fully cooked spicy chicken sausage, sliced

2   carrots, thinly sliced

2   small zucchini, sliced

1   can (about 15 ounces) Great Northern, cannellini or navy beans, rinsed and drained

2   tablespoons chopped fresh basil (optional)

SLOW COOKER DIRECTIONS

1. Combine all ingredients except beans and basil in slow cooker. Cover; cook on LOW 6 to 7 hours or on HIGH 3 to 4 hours or until vegetables are tender.

2. *Turn slow cooker to HIGH.* Stir in beans. Cover; cook 10 to 15 minutes or until beans are heated through. Ladle into shallow bowls; top with basil, if desired.

Makes 4 servings

CAJUN CHILI

1½ pounds ground beef

2 cans (about 15 ounces each) Cajun-style mixed vegetables

2 cans (10¾ ounces each) condensed tomato soup

1 can (about 14 ounces) diced tomatoes

3 sausages with Cheddar cheese (about 8 ounces), cut into bite-size pieces

Shredded Cheddar cheese (optional)

SLOW COOKER DIRECTIONS

1. Brown beef in large skillet over medium-high heat 6 to 8 minutes, stirring to break up meat. Drain fat.

2. Place beef, mixed vegetables, soup, tomatoes and sausages in slow cooker.

3. Cover; cook on HIGH 2 to 3 hours. Top with cheese, if desired.

Makes 10 servings

ITALIAN SAUSAGE AND VEGETABLE STEW

1 pound hot or mild
   Italian sausage
   links, cut into 1-inch
   pieces

1 package (16 ounces)
   frozen vegetable
   blend, such as
   onions and bell
   peppers

2 medium zucchini,
   sliced

1 can (about 14 ounces)
   Italian-style diced
   tomatoes

1 can (4 ounces) sliced
   mushrooms, drained

4 cloves garlic, minced

1. Brown sausage in large saucepan over medium-high heat 5 minutes, stirring frequently; drain fat.

2. Add frozen vegetables, zucchini, tomatoes, mushrooms and garlic; bring to a boil. Reduce heat to medium-low; cover and simmer 10 minutes. Cook, uncovered, 5 to 10 minutes or until thickened slightly.

Makes 6 servings

5-MINUTE HEAT-AND-GO SOUP

1   can (about 15 ounces) navy beans, rinsed and drained

1   can (about 14 ounces) diced tomatoes with green peppers and onions

1   cup water

1½ teaspoons dried basil

½   teaspoon sugar

½   teaspoon chicken bouillon granules

2   teaspoons olive oil

1. Place all ingredients except oil in medium saucepan; bring to a boil over high heat. Reduce heat and simmer 5 minutes, uncovered. Remove from heat; stir in oil.

2. If desired, to transport, place hot soup in vacuum flask or allow to cool and place in a plastic container. Reheat in microwave when needed.

Makes 3½ cups (about 4 servings)

HAMBURGER VEGGIE SOUP

1 pound ground beef

1 bag (16 ounces) frozen mixed vegetables

1 bag (10 ounces) frozen seasoning blend vegetables

1 can (about 14 ounces) stewed tomatoes, undrained

2 cans (5½ ounces each) spicy vegetable juice

1 can (10¾ ounces) condensed tomato soup, undiluted

Salt and black pepper

SLOW COOKER DIRECTIONS

1. Brown beef in large skillet over medium-high heat 6 to 8 minutes, stirring to break up meat. Drain fat.

2. Combine beef, vegetables, tomatoes, juice and soup in slow cooker. Stir well.

3. Cover; cook on HIGH 4 hours. Season with salt and pepper.

Makes 4 to 6 servings

QUICK AND ZESTY VEGETABLE SOUP

1   lb. lean ground beef
½   cup chopped onion
    Salt and pepper
2   cans (14.5 oz. each)
    DEL MONTE® Italian
    Recipe Stewed
    Tomatoes
2   cans (14 oz. each) beef
    broth
1   can (14.5 oz.) DEL
    MONTE® Mixed
    Vegetables
½   cup uncooked
    medium egg noodles
½   tsp. dried oregano

1. Brown meat with onion in large saucepan. Cook until onion is tender; drain. Season to taste with salt and pepper.

2. Stir in remaining ingredients. Bring to boil; reduce heat.

3. Cover and simmer 15 minutes or until noodles are tender.

Makes 8 servings

SKILLET SOUTHWEST CHILI

1 lb. lean ground beef

2 cans (14.5 oz. each) DEL MONTE® Diced Tomatoes with Onion and Garlic

1 can (15 oz.) low-sodium black or kidney beans, rinsed and drained

1 can (4 oz.) diced green chiles

1 Tbsp. chili powder

Green onions or cilantro (optional)

1. Brown beef in large skillet; drain.

2. Add undrained tomatoes, beans, chiles and chili powder; simmer 10 minutes, stirring occasionally. Garnish with green onions, if desired.

Makes 4 servings

SUMMER SQUASH STEW

2 pounds bulk Italian
  turkey sausage
  or diced cooked
  chicken

4 cans (about
  14 ounces each)
  diced seasoned
  tomatoes, undrained

5 medium yellow
  squash, thinly sliced

5 medium zucchini,
  thinly sliced

1 red onion, finely
  chopped

2 tablespoons Italian
  seasoning

1 tablespoon dried
  tomato, basil and
  garlic salt-free spice
  seasoning

4 cups (16 ounces)
  shredded Mexican
  cheese blend

SLOW COOKER DIRECTIONS

1. Brown sausage in batches in large
nonstick skillet over medium-
high heat, stirring to break up
meat. Drain fat. Combine sausage,
tomatoes with juice, squash,
zucchini, onion and seasonings
in 4-quart slow cooker; mix well.
Cover; cook on LOW 3 hours.

2. Serve with cheese.

Makes 6 servings

CHUNKY CHICKEN STEW

1 teaspoon olive oil

1 small onion, chopped

1 cup thinly sliced carrots

1 cup chicken broth

1 can (about 14 ounces) diced tomatoes

1 cup diced cooked chicken breast

3 cups sliced kale or baby spinach

1. Heat oil in large saucepan over medium-high heat. Add onion; cook and stir about 5 minutes or until golden brown. Stir in carrots and broth; bring to a boil. Reduce heat; simmer, uncovered, 5 minutes.

2. Stir in tomatoes; simmer 5 minutes or until carrots are tender. Add chicken; cook and stir until heated through. Add kale; stir until wilted.

Makes 2 servings

MINESTRONE SOUP

¾ cup uncooked small shell pasta

2 cans (about 14 ounces each) vegetable broth

1 can (28 ounces) crushed tomatoes in tomato purée

1 can (about 15 ounces) white beans, rinsed and drained

1 package (16 ounces) frozen vegetable medley, such as broccoli, green beans, carrots and red peppers

4 to 6 teaspoons prepared pesto

1. Cook pasta according to package directions. Drain.

2. Meanwhile, combine broth, tomatoes and beans in Dutch oven. Cover and bring to a boil over high heat. Reduce heat to low; simmer 3 to 5 minutes.

3. Add vegetables to broth mixture and return to a boil over high heat. Stir in pasta. Simmer until vegetables and pasta are tender. Ladle soup into bowls; spoon about 1 teaspoon pesto in center of each serving.

Makes 4 to 6 servings

KICK'N CHILI

2 pounds ground beef

1 tablespoon *each* salt, ground cumin, chili powder, paprika, dried oregano and black pepper

2 teaspoons red pepper flakes

2 cloves garlic, minced

¼ teaspoon ground red pepper

3 cans (about 10 ounces each) diced tomatoes with mild green chiles

1 jar (about 16 ounces) salsa

1 onion, chopped

SLOW COOKER DIRECTIONS

1. Combine beef, salt, cumin, chili powder, paprika, oregano, black pepper, red pepper flakes, garlic and ground red pepper in large bowl.

2. Brown beef in large skillet over medium-high heat 6 to 8 minutes, stirring to break up meat. Drain fat. Add tomatoes, salsa and onion; mix well. Transfer beef mixture to slow cooker. Cover; cook on LOW 4 to 6 hours.

Makes 6 servings

 TIP: This chunky chili is very spicy. Reduce red pepper flakes for a milder flavor.

SALADS & SIDES

GINGERSNAP SWEET POTATO FOOL

1 can (15 ounces) sweet potato purée *or* 2 cups cooked, puréed sweet potatoes

¼ cup packed light brown sugar

½ teaspoon ground cinnamon

¼ teaspoon ground ginger

1 cup whipping cream

3 tablespoons powdered sugar

12 gingersnap cookies, coarsely crushed

1. Combine sweet potatoes, brown sugar, cinnamon and ginger in medium bowl, stirring until well blended.

2. Beat cream in large bowl with electric mixer at high speed until thickened. Gradually add powdered sugar; beat until stiff.

3. To assemble, layer half of gingersnaps in 2-quart glass bowl. Spread with half of sweet potato purée and half of whipped cream. Repeat layers. Chill 1 hour before serving.

Makes 6 servings

 TIP: Coarsely crushed cookies give this fool a crunchy texture. If you prefer, crush cookies finely instead.

SPANISH RICE WITH CHORIZO

4 links Spanish-style chorizo sausage (about 12 ounces), thinly sliced diagonally

1 green bell pepper, diced

1½ cups uncooked instant rice

1 can (about 14 ounces) diced tomatoes

1 cup chicken broth *or* water

2 green onions, chopped

Salt and black pepper

1. Cook and stir sausage and bell pepper in large nonstick skillet over medium heat 5 minutes or until bell pepper is tender. Stir in rice, tomatoes, broth and green onions.

2. Increase heat to high. Bring to a boil. Reduce heat to medium-low; cover and simmer 8 to 10 minutes or until liquid is absorbed and rice is tender. Season with salt and black pepper.

Makes 4 servings

NOTE: For a vegetarian version, substitute soy-based sausages for the chorizo and add 1 tablespoon vegetable oil to the skillet with the sausages and bell pepper. Substitute vegetable broth or water for the chicken broth.

BROCCOLI PESCETORE

1 jar (26 ounces)
   marinara pasta
   sauce

1 can (about 15 ounces)
   white beans, rinsed
   and drained

1 can (6 ounces) tuna
   packed in water,
   drained and flaked

1 tablespoon chopped
   or minced garlic

2 teaspoons dried
   oregano

1 bag (12 ounces) frozen
   broccoli florets,
   prepared according
   to package
   directions

¼ cup grated Parmesan
   cheese

   Black pepper

1. Combine pasta sauce, beans, tuna, garlic and oregano in medium saucepan. Cook over medium-high heat about 6 minutes or until heated through.

2. Divide broccoli among four pasta bowls. Garnish with cheese. Season with pepper.

Makes 4 servings

MEXICAN-STYLE RICE AND CHEESE

1 can (about 15 ounces)
  Mexican-style beans

1 can (about 14 ounces)
  diced tomatoes with
  mild green chiles

2 cups (8 ounces)
  shredded Monterey
  Jack or Colby
  cheese, divided

1½ cups uncooked
  converted long grain
  rice

1 large onion, finely
  chopped

½ of an 8-ounce
  package cream
  cheese

3 cloves garlic, minced

SLOW COOKER DIRECTIONS

1. Spray inside of slow cooker with nonstick cooking spray. Combine beans, tomatoes, 1 cup Monterey Jack cheese, rice, onion, cream cheese and garlic in slow cooker; mix well. Cover; cook on LOW 6 to 8 hours.

2. Sprinkle with remaining 1 cup Monterey Jack cheese just before serving.

Makes 6 to 8 servings

SOUTHWEST SPAGHETTI SQUASH

1 spaghetti squash (about 3 pounds), cut in half length-wise and seeds removed

1 can (about 14 ounces) Mexican-style diced tomatoes

1 can (about 14 ounces) black beans, rinsed and drained

¾ cup (3 ounces) shredded Monterey Jack cheese, divided

¼ cup finely chopped fresh cilantro

1 teaspoon ground cumin

¼ teaspoon garlic salt

¼ teaspoon black pepper

1. Preheat oven to 350°F.

2. Spray baking sheet and 1½-quart baking dish with nonstick cooking spray. Place squash, cut side down, on prepared baking sheet.

3. Bake 45 minutes or just until tender. Shred squash with fork; place in large bowl. (Use oven mitts to protect hands.) Add tomatoes, beans, ½ cup cheese, cilantro, cumin, garlic salt and pepper; toss well. Spoon mixture into prepared baking dish. Sprinkle with remaining ¼ cup cheese.

4. Bake 30 to 35 minutes or until heated through.

Makes 4 servings

 TIP: This is a very simple, "kid-friendly" dish you can throw together in just a few minutes. It's great for those nights you want to go meatless!

ITALIAN GREEN BEAN SAUTÉ

½ small onion, cut into thin wedges

1 small clove garlic, minced

½ tsp. dried basil

1 Tbsp. olive oil

2 cans (14.5 oz. each) DEL MONTE® Cut Green Beans-No Salt Added, drained

1 can (14.5 oz.) DEL MONTE® Petite Diced Tomatoes, drained

1. Cook onion, garlic and basil in oil in medium saucepan over medium heat, 5 minutes or until onion is tender.

2. Add green beans and tomatoes; heat through.

Makes 6 servings

TIP: Watching your sodium intake? Use *DEL MONTE*® 50% Less Salt Cut Green Beans or *DEL MONTE*® No Salt Added Cut Green Beans and *DEL MONTE*® No Salt Added Diced Tomatoes.

MEDITERRANEAN PASTA SALAD

12 ounces uncooked
   rotini pasta

1 bottle (8 ounces)
   Italian vinaigrette,
   divided

1 can (about 6 ounces)
   tuna packed in
   water, drained

3 hard-cooked eggs,
   peeled and cut into
   wedges

1 cup frozen green
   beans, thawed

¼ cup pitted black
   olives

1. Cook pasta according to package directions; drain.

2. Reserve ¼ cup vinaigrette. Toss pasta with remaining vinaigrette; place on serving platter or on individual plates.

3. Arrange tuna, eggs, green beans and olives on top of pasta. Drizzle with reserved vinaigrette. Serve chilled or at room temperature.

Makes 6 servings

 TIP: Serve with an easy, flavor-boosting garnish: parsley-dipped lemon wedges. Place parsley in small bowl and dip cut edge of each lemon wedge into parsley to coat lemon.

ORIENTAL PILAF

1 tablespoon vegetable oil

1 cup chopped onion

2 cloves garlic, minced

1 cup uncooked rice

1 can (about 14 ounces) chicken broth

¼ cup water*

3 ounces (1 cup) fresh snow peas, cut lengthwise into thin strips

2 medium carrots, coarsely shredded

*If using converted rice, increase water to ½ cup.

1. Heat oil in medium saucepan over medium heat. Add onion and garlic; cook and stir 4 minutes or until tender. Add rice; cook and stir 1 minute.

2. Add broth and water. Bring to a boil over high heat. Reduce heat to low. Cover and simmer 18 minutes. Stir in snow peas and carrots. Cover and simmer 2 minutes or until liquid is absorbed.

3. Remove from heat. Let stand, covered, 5 minutes; fluff with fork before serving.

Makes 4 servings

BEANS WITH SMOKY CANADIAN BACON

2   cans (about 14 ounces each) diced fire-roasted tomatoes

1   can (about 15 ounces) pinto beans, rinsed and drained

1   package (8 ounces) Canadian bacon, cut into ½-inch cubes

½   cup Texas-style barbecue sauce*

1   onion, finely chopped

½   teaspoon salt

Black pepper

⅛   teaspoon red pepper flakes (optional)

*Look for barbecue sauce with liquid smoke as an ingredient.

SLOW COOKER DIRECTIONS

Combine all ingredients in slow cooker. Cover; cook on LOW 5 to 7 hours. Serve in bowls.

Makes 4 servings

ZESTY PASTA SALAD

1 cup (about 3 ounces) uncooked tri-color rotini pasta

1 cup sliced mushrooms

¾ cup canned diced tomatoes

½ cup sliced green bell pepper

¼ cup chopped onion

¼ cup Italian salad dressing

2 tablespoons freshly grated Parmesan cheese

Fresh lettuce leaves (optional)

1. Cook pasta according to package directions. Rinse under cool running water. Drain; cool completely.

2. Combine pasta, mushrooms, tomatoes, bell pepper and onion in large bowl. Pour Italian dressing over pasta mixture; toss to coat evenly. Sprinkle with cheese just before serving. Serve over lettuce, if desired.

Makes 6 servings

DOWN-HOME SQUASH CASSEROLE

4 cups corn bread stuffing mix (½ of 16-ounce package)

½ cup (1 stick) butter, melted

1 can (10¾ ounces) condensed cream of chicken soup, undiluted

¾ cup mayonnaise

¼ cup milk

¼ teaspoon poultry seasoning or rubbed sage

3 medium yellow squash (about 1 pound total), cut into ½-inch slices

1½ cups frozen seasoning blend vegetables, thawed*

*Seasoning blend is a mixture of chopped bell peppers, onions and celery. If seasoning blend is unavailable, use ½ cup each of fresh vegetables.

SLOW COOKER DIRECTIONS

1. Coat 5-quart slow cooker with nonstick cooking spray. Combine stuffing and butter in large bowl; toss gently to coat stuffing thoroughly. Place ⅔ of stuffing in slow cooker. Place remaining stuffing on plate; set aside.

2. Combine soup, mayonnaise, milk and poultry seasoning in same large bowl. Add squash and vegetables; stir until coated thoroughly. Pour mixture over stuffing mix in slow cooker. Sprinkle with reserved stuffing. Cover; cook on LOW 4 hours or until squash is tender.

3. Turn off slow cooker. Uncover and let stand 15 minutes before serving.

Makes 8 to 10 servings

SCALLOPED TOMATOES & CORN

1 can (15 ounces)
cream-style corn

1 can (about 14 ounces)
diced tomatoes

¾ cup saltine cracker
crumbs

1 egg, lightly beaten

2 teaspoons sugar

¾ teaspoon black
pepper

Chopped fresh
tomatoes (optional)

Chopped fresh Italian
parsley (optional)

SLOW COOKER DIRECTIONS

1. Combine corn, diced tomatoes, cracker crumbs, egg, sugar and pepper in slow cooker; mix well.

2. Cover; cook on LOW 4 to 6 hours. Sprinkle with tomatoes and parsley before serving, if desired.

Makes 4 to 6 servings

SIMPLE SUMMER PASTA SALAD

8 ounces uncooked bow tie pasta

2 large tomatoes, seeded and chopped

1 package (8 ounces) fresh mozzarella cheese, cut into ½-inch pieces

1 can (6 ounces) tuna packed in water, drained

⅓ cup coarsely chopped fresh basil

1 clove garlic, minced

¾ cup Italian dressing

Black pepper

1. Cook pasta according to package directions; drain.

2. Combine tomatoes, cheese, tuna, basil and garlic in large bowl; toss gently. Add pasta and dressing; toss lightly to coat. Season with pepper. Refrigerate before serving.

Makes 6 to 8 servings

SNACKS & DESSERTS

RAMEN JOY

1¼ cups sweetened shredded coconut

1 package (3 ounces) ramen noodles, any flavor, crushed*

½ cup slivered almonds, coarsely chopped

¾ cup sweetened condensed milk

¾ teaspoon vanilla

¼ teaspoon salt

¾ cup powdered sugar

8 ounces chocolate candy coating

*Discard seasoning packet.

1. Line bottom and sides of 13×9-inch baking pan with foil. Lightly coat with nonstick cooking spray.

2. Heat large nonstick skillet over medium heat. Add coconut, ramen noodles and almonds; cook 3 to 5 minutes or until slightly golden brown in color, stirring frequently. Remove from heat.

3. Stir in condensed milk, vanilla and salt until well blended. Stir in powdered sugar. Fold in noodle mixture until thick paste consistency is reached. Spread mixture onto foil in prepared pan to approximately ¼-inch thickness.

4. Melt chocolate according to package directions. Spread chocolate evenly over noodle mixture. Place in freezer 15 minutes to firm slightly. Cut into pieces.

Makes 32 pieces

PUMPKIN PIE TRIFLE

2 cups canned pumpkin pie mix

1½ cups whipping cream

1 prepared angel food cake, cut into 1-inch cubes

Fall sprinkles (optional)

1. Place pumpkin pie mix in medium bowl.

2. Beat whipping cream in large bowl until stiff peaks form. Spoon one-third of whipped cream into pumpkin pie mix; fold with spatula until blended. Add another one third of whipped cream to pumpkin mixture; fold with spatula until uniform in color. Reserve remaining one third of whipped cream for garnish.

3. Layer cake cubes and pumpkin mixture in deep glass bowl, beginning and ending with pumpkin mixture. Garnish with reserved whipped cream and sprinkles.

Makes 8 to 10 servings

PEANUT BUTTER COOKIE BARS

- 1 package (18 ounces) refrigerated peanut butter cookie dough
- 1 can (14 ounces) sweetened condensed milk
- ¼ cup all-purpose flour
- ¼ cup peanut butter
- 1 cup peanut butter chips
- 1 cup chopped peanuts

1. Preheat oven to 350°F. Lightly grease 13×9-inch baking pan. Let dough stand at room temperature about 15 minutes.

2. Press dough evenly onto bottom of prepared pan. Bake 10 minutes.

3. Meanwhile, combine sweetened condensed milk, flour and peanut butter in medium bowl; beat until well blended. Spoon over partially baked crust. Sprinkle evenly with peanut butter chips and peanuts; press down lightly.

4. Bake 15 to 18 minutes or until center is set. Cool completely in pan on wire rack.

Makes about 2 dozen bars

CHOCOLATE PEANUT BUTTER CANDY BARS

1 package (about 18 ounces) devil's food or dark chocolate cake mix *without* pudding in the mix

1 can (5 ounces) evaporated milk

⅓ cup butter, melted

½ cup dry-roasted peanuts

4 packages (1½ ounces each) chocolate peanut butter cups, coarsely chopped

1. Preheat oven to 350°F. Lightly grease 13×9-inch baking pan.

2. Beat cake mix, evaporated milk and butter in large bowl with electric mixer at medium speed until well blended. (Dough will be stiff.) Press two thirds of dough into bottom of prepared pan. Sprinkle with peanuts.

3. Bake 10 minutes; sprinkle with chopped candy. Drop remaining dough by large tablespoonfuls over top. Bake 15 to 20 minutes or until center is firm to the touch. Cool completely in pan on wire rack.

Makes about 2 dozen bars

EASY LEMON CHEESECAKE

2 packages (8 ounces each) cream cheese, softened

1 can (14 ounces) sweetened condensed milk (not evaporated milk)

3 eggs

¼ cup lemon juice

1 (9-ounce) graham cracker crust

1 container (8 ounces) sour cream

Assorted cut-up fruit

1. Preheat oven to 325°F.

2. Beat cream cheese and condensed milk in large bowl with electric mixer at medium speed until well blended. Add eggs and lemon juice; beat just until blended. Pour into crust.

3. Bake 40 minutes or until set. Remove from oven; spread sour cream over cheesecake. Bake 5 minutes. Cool on wire rack. Refrigerate 3 hours or overnight. Top with fruit just before serving.

Makes 6 to 8 servings

POWER-PACKED PUMPKIN POTS

1 can (15 ounces) solid-pack pumpkin

1 can (12 ounces) evaporated milk

3 eggs

½ cup sugar

1 teaspoon pumpkin pie spice*

1 teaspoon vanilla

½ teaspoon salt

Whipped cream (optional)

*Or substitute ½ teaspoon ground cinnamon, ¼ teaspoon ground ginger, ⅛ teaspoon ground allspice and ⅛ teaspoon ground nutmeg.

1. Preheat oven to 350°F. Spray 6 to 8 (4-ounce) custard cups or ramekins with nonstick cooking spray.

2. Combine pumpkin, evaporated milk, eggs, sugar, pumpkin pie spice, vanilla and salt in large bowl. Whisk until thoroughly blended.

3. Pour mixture evenly into prepared custard cups; place in baking pan. Pour hot water into pan around cups to depth of 1 inch. Carefully place baking pan in oven.

4. Bake 1 hour or until knife inserted into center comes out clean.

5. Remove custard cups to wire rack. Let stand 30 minutes. Refrigerate 1 to 2 hours or overnight. Serve with whipped cream, if desired.

Makes 6 to 8 servings

NUTTY CHOCOLATE OAT BARS

1 cup all-purpose flour
1 cup old-fashioned oats
¾ cup firmly packed brown sugar
½ cup (1 stick) butter, softened
1 can (14 ounces) sweetened condensed milk
1 cup chopped walnuts or pecans
1 cup semisweet chocolate chips

1. Preheat oven to 350°F. Combine flour, oats, brown sugar and butter in large bowl; mix until ingredients are crumbly. Reserve ½ cup mixture. Press remaining mixture firmly on bottom of ungreased 13×9-inch baking pan. Bake 10 minutes. Remove from oven.

2. Spread condensed milk evenly over crust. Sprinkle evenly with nuts and chocolate chips. Sprinkle reserved oat mixture evenly over top; press down firmly.

3. Bake 25 minutes or until lightly browned. Cool completely on wire rack. Cut into bars.

Makes 2 to 3 dozen bars

PUMPKIN SPICE MUG CAKE

¼ cup angel food cake mix

3 tablespoons water

2 teaspoons solid-pack canned pumpkin

1 teaspoon finely chopped pecans

¼ teaspoon pumpkin pie spice

MICROWAVE DIRECTIONS

1. Combine cake mix, water, pumpkin, pecans and pumpkin pie spice in large ceramic* microwavable mug; mix well.

2. Microwave on HIGH 2 minutes. Let stand 1 to 2 minutes before serving.

This cake will only work in a ceramic mug as the material allows for more even cooking than glass.

Makes 1 serving

ACKNOWLEDGMENTS

The publisher would like to thank the companies listed below for the use of their recipes and photographs in this publication.

Del Monte Foods®
Dole Food Company, Inc.
Hormel Foods, The Makers of Hormel® Chunk Meats
Nestlé USA
Pinnacle Foods
Unilever

METRIC CONVERSION CHART

VOLUME MEASUREMENTS (dry)

$^1/_8$ teaspoon = 0.5 mL
$^1/_4$ teaspoon = 1 mL
$^1/_2$ teaspoon = 2 mL
$^3/_4$ teaspoon = 4 mL
1 teaspoon = 5 mL
1 tablespoon = 15 mL
2 tablespoons = 30 mL
$^1/_4$ cup = 60 mL
$^1/_3$ cup = 75 mL
$^1/_2$ cup = 125 mL
$^2/_3$ cup = 150 mL
$^3/_4$ cup = 175 mL
1 cup = 250 mL
2 cups = 1 pint = 500 mL
3 cups = 750 mL
4 cups = 1 quart = 1 L

VOLUME MEASUREMENTS (fluid)

1 fluid ounce (2 tablespoons) = 30 mL
4 fluid ounces ($^1/_2$ cup) = 125 mL
8 fluid ounces (1 cup) = 250 mL
12 fluid ounces (1$^1/_2$ cups) = 375 mL
16 fluid ounces (2 cups) = 500 mL

WEIGHTS (mass)

$^1/_2$ ounce = 15 g
1 ounce = 30 g
3 ounces = 90 g
4 ounces = 120 g
8 ounces = 225 g
10 ounces = 285 g
12 ounces = 360 g
16 ounces = 1 pound = 450 g

DIMENSIONS

$^1/_{16}$ inch = 2 mm
$^1/_8$ inch = 3 mm
$^1/_4$ inch = 6 mm
$^1/_2$ inch = 1.5 cm
$^3/_4$ inch = 2 cm
1 inch = 2.5 cm

OVEN TEMPERATURES

250°F = 120°C
275°F = 140°C
300°F = 150°C
325°F = 160°C
350°F = 180°C
375°F = 190°C
400°F = 200°C
425°F = 220°C
450°F = 230°C

BAKING PAN SIZES

Utensil	Size in Inches/Quarts	Metric Volume	Size in Centimeters
Baking or Cake Pan (square or rectangular)	8×8×2	2 L	20×20×5
	9×9×2	2.5 L	23×23×5
	12×8×2	3 L	30×20×5
	13×9×2	3.5 L	33×23×5
Loaf Pan	8×4×3	1.5 L	20×10×7
	9×5×3	2 L	23×13×7
Round Layer Cake Pan	8×1½	1.2 L	20×4
	9×1½	1.5 L	23×4
Pie Plate	8×1¼	750 mL	20×3
	9×1¼	1 L	23×3
Baking Dish or Casserole	1 quart	1 L	—
	1½ quart	1.5 L	—
	2 quart	2 L	—